Real Estate Investing

How to Quit Your Job and Live in Wealth Through Real Estate Investments

Table of Contents

Table of Contents 3
Introduction 5
Real Estate Investing 101 9
Budgets, Banks, and Borrowing 28
Types of Investing 55
Turn-Key Cash Flow 78
How to Locate Properties 93
for Cash Flow 93
Seller Information Sheet 127
Overcoming Challenges and Quitting Your Day Job 130
Conclusion 149
BONUS MATERIALS 154

Introduction

Well Hello! Welcome to the world of real estate investing!

This book is designed to give you a good understanding of how to get started, setting up business formation, marketing, different ways to use funds, present different investment strategies, learn about budgets, what options are available to get involve in partnership, how to overcome challenges and set it up so you can fire your boss, and quit your day job!

I can say confidently that real estate investing can be life-changing. You can invest with all budgets, work part or full time, replace your income, retire, and enjoy the life you WANT not the life you need to survive. The best thing about real estate investing is that it requires no formal degree of education, is open to all economic classes, all races, and genders can be used not only nationwide but worldwide, and anyone can learn the techniques to generate the cash flow they desire.

Use this book like it is a tool for your toolbox. Take notes, highlight, re-read, and use the information to make a change in your life. There will be techniques you can use as your business grows and forms that you use to foster the growth you experience. Each section can be used and duplicated so that you can reproduce and create your own level of success. The information is meant to be universal and be modified to fit your specific geographic area and the type of investing you prefer to generate cash flow. Some portions of this book are informational, some are technical, and some are going to require interacting and implementing physical activities to help you better learn and understand real estate investing. But used as a whole, the information in the following pages can help you reach the financial goals you are looking for. Not one person will use this information the same way and that is what it is designed for - for you, the investor, to create your own world of investing with a few simple techniques.

So, congratulations on taking the steps needed to join the elite group of Real estate investors. More millionaires are made every day in one form of real estate or another and you deserve to be a part of the Millionaire's club. Move forward knowing that real estate investing can create a lifestyle where you live life on your own terms.

People always say that knowledge is power - but that is not true - knowledge is NOT power. Knowledge is POWERFUL! But it is only powerful if you use it and implement that knowledge to create results for your actions. Success is not a guarantee but it is an option if you choose to make it an option.

Real Estate Investing 101

Real estate investing is a world where the income potential is unlimited and cash flow comes in 24 hours a day, 7 days a week, 365 days a year. Yes, welcome to real estate investing!

If you are here, then the Real Estate bug has bitten you and you likely have thought about getting into Real Estate investing for some time, but have just never taken the steps needed to start or maybe you just don't know which direction to go to reach the ideas you have. This is the place to jump-start that process.

In this chapter, we are going to cover some beginning technical items to help get you started on the right track. We are going to help you understand the real "WHY" behind your desire to be a real estate investor, organize and create goal-setting options, how to get a business set up, and how to market yourself. So, let's get going!

"WHY?"

Like any venture, there has to be a reason why you want to get involved in it. What prompted that idea to keep coming back into your thoughts and finally push you to take the first step in getting started?

So, I would ask you, "Why do you want to get into real estate investing?"

I'm sure you have a quick answer that is easy to share, right?

"To make more money!"
"Go on the vacation of my dreams"
"Give my kids the life I never had"

Don't get me wrong, these are GREAT and can be the results of real estate investing but again… "WHY do you want to get into Real Estate Investing?"

What is the deep, soul pressing reason that will get you up every day to push through the countless hours of running numbers, viewing properties, rehabbing, dealing with contractors, losing money, collecting rent, fixing repairs, and more?

Once you peel back the onion, so to speak, you will begin to understand the driving force behind your desire to start investing in Real Estate. The next exercise is designed to help you map out "WHY" and give you clarity. Without a real "WHY", you have no connection to things needed to help you get where you want to be. I know it looks crazy, but trust the process and systems that have been used by most, if not all, of the highly successful real estate investors.

I want to be a Successful Real Estate Investor Because:

1)_____

But why 2)_____

But why 3)_____

But why 4)_____

But why 5)_____

But why 6)_____

But why 7)_____

But why 8) _____

Are you surprised by your "WHY"? Work through the exercise above and be honest. Maybe, by the end, you discover that it is because you lived in your car as a child because your house burned down and your family couldn't afford a new home for a while and you refuse to let that happen to your family, or maybe your family struggled due to unforeseen financial challenges when you were young and you want to make sure that you never wonder whether the money will be there or not. Maybe none of your family has ever had the chance at college and you want to make sure that is an option for your children. There is no right or wrong answers but get serious with yourself and take some time and really thing about WHY you give the answers your give.

Did you struggle to admit some of those things that you hold close and make yourself vulnerable? If so, good job on opening up and allowing yourself to see the real reason why you want to have success and invest in real estate. This will help you, in the long run, to stay the course and see it through till the end.

Now you know your "WHY", let's talk about putting things in perspective and start some goal setting so that "WHY" comes to fruition.

Goals and Goal Setting

Benjamin Franklin said, "By failing to prepare, you are preparing to fail."

A business without a plan can't grow. It may flounder along and have some success but it will not reach its true potential. The key point is if you don't have goals or a formal business and you just have a hobby. Setting up realistic and obtainable goals will help you move forward methodically and reach small steps of success which lead to big steps of success which leads to goal accomplishments.

Earlier in this chapter, we discovered your "Why". The one thing that will keep you going even when business gets tough. Now, we need to talk about setting up a systematic approach to daily, weekly, monthly, and annual activities to stay on track and make things happen. You can buy a binder or notebook to write down your goals or you can post them on sticky notes, it doesn't matter. What matters is that you write them down. Writing them down makes them real, you can visualize them better, see them on a regular basis, and they become engrained in your memory which makes them something you strive to reach.

I would suggest starting off by just doing a brain dump. This is where you just start writing things you would like to achieve in life that you feel Real Estate Investing will allow you to do. In no particular order, write what type of investing you want to do, how many properties you want to be involved in, how many rentals you want to own, if you want to own multi-family property, buy a new house, pay for your kid's college - this is YOUR list, so think about it and write it down.

Once you have it all dumped on to paper, go back through and start organizing it. Separate it by business goals and by personal goals achieved by the real estate success.

An example would be:

GOALS

Buy 1 property in 30 days to flip

Buy 2nd flip in 45 days

Buy 1 property to keep as rental in 6 months

PERSONAL GOALS

Buy a new house

Buy work vehicle

Retire early from JOB

Once this is done, take the Goal's side and make notes underneath each line item and note the steps needed to reach that one specific goal. Do each one and they can be as elaborate as needed. Do not take shortcuts on the steps or you will change the goal.

Then take the Personal Goal's side and do the same. Keep in mind that the steps taken on this side will need to be a result of the goals reached on the Goal side.

<u>GOALS</u>

- Buy 1 property in 30 days to flip

    - Week 1
        - Set up a marketing plan
        - Send out Marketing and advertise in 3 places in the next 7 days to find a property
        - Attend an investment club meeting to meet sellers, rehabbers, property managers...

- Week 2
    - Work marketing plan
    - Call back property owners and set up viewings of potential houses to buy
    - Run numbers on houses to see if they fit by criteria
- Week 3
    - Make an offer on a property
    - Set up financing or arrange for Cash transfer

PERSONAL GOALS
- Buy a New House
    - Complete 3 flips for down payment
    - Have 2 cash flowing rentals

These are just examples but you see how the Personal goals are reflective of the results of your

GOALS. Once you reach those goals, you can begin to cash in on the Personal goals.

Goal setting is not a one-and-done activity. This needs to be done at least quarterly so that you are staying on top of the forward movement and flow of your business. As your business grows, so will the goals you had set or they may change if you learn something new or don't like a particular avenue of investing. Regardless, note the ones you meet and keep setting new ones to keep the momentum moving in your business. Once you achieve a goal or two, you will find that reaching a goal and getting what you wanted is a huge motivator so don't ever stop planning and goal setting.

Business Formation

I want to reassure you that you do not need to have any special degree to invest in real estate. You do not need to have a Real Estate license. You don't need a college degree nor do you need to have completed high school. Real estate investing is easy to learn. It is a repeatable and duplicable process that can be done by anyone anywhere who is committed to implementing what they are taught.

Since there are several ways to make cash flow in real estate, it is important that you have a business entity set up to help you operate on an official level for yourself and your clients. Setting up a formal business also allows you to hire employees easier, gives you tax benefits and write-offs, and allows to minimize loss easier. One of the main reasons for operating under a business entity is so that you have the opportunity to personally remain separate from your business.

To get an entity set up you first need to think about what you want to call your business. There are a lot of philosophies about how to name a business and how not to and you need to decide for yourself what you feel is right for you. What I can suggest is that you 1) not use your name and 2) make sure you indicate what you do but not too specific or vague. When considering a business name, you want it to be easy to speak and read, short and to the point, easy to spell - especially if you create an online presence - and that looks good on your marketing materials.

Some not so good examples:
1) Barker Real Estate – Uses a personal name, real estate is a vague description of what you may be doing.
2) Maxon Homes- Again personal name usages and "Homes" could imply you are a builder, manufacturer, Realtor...
3) Bakauta House Flipping - Personal name - difficult to pronounce and spell and limits you to 1 form of investing -Flipping.

Some good name examples:
1) Midnight Investment Properties - No personal name used and it indicates you are associated with Investment Properties.
2) Right Time Home Investors - Again no personal name but gives clients sense that you are there at the "Right Time" and that you are a Home Investor

3) Platinum Commercial Property Investments – Platinum - is a Good Strong Metal – indicating the high value and this name lets people know you invest in the Commercial Property Space

A lot of people ask if they should set up their entity as an LLC, Sole Proprietor, S-corp, or an LLP, and although we cannot suggest one over the other, we do encourage you to consult an attorney or Real Estate minded CPA who can advise you on which entity type makes the most sense for your business goals and needs. Again you just want to make sure that your business name is clear, easy to say, and lets your clients know what you do so they can find you when they need you.

Marketing

Aside from getting a business entity set up, I would say that Marketing is the next most important thing to do. Let's face it, if no one knows you're in business, your business doesn't exist. Letting people know you are in business is how to start to generate cash flow. Marketing can be fun, easy, and very inexpensive, or as you grow, you can start increasing and add a marketing budget.

The first thing to do is to get some business cards. No, they are not overrated or outdated. They are easy to carry and hand out and they fit in potential clients' pockets for them to pull out at a later time and remember who you were and why they needed to call you. On your first order, don't order too many because you will see that you will want to modify them at least once after you get them and physically see them in your hands. You may want to add a logo or photo and by buying a small amount initially, you can make an adjustment if needed and still be economical. You can make business cards yourself by using a label program online and buying the business card stock at a local office supply. Or you can order them online from any company that offers business card services or a local print show. There are some online companies that offer FREE cards if you just pay the shipping on your first order, so shop around and be mindful of your spending to get things set up. Although you will be able to use these as business expense write-offs, they don't need to be high-end and super fancy.

Social Media is a huge option and it would be smart to use it to its full advantage. It is free to set up business pages off of your standard Facebook social media page. A unique part of Facebook is that you can join groups of like-minded people and network in your community with people you have not yet met. You can introduce yourself and what you do and ask if anyone wants to buy investment properties or can refer you to someone who may. When you are all set up on Facebook with your business page, you can also advertise yourself for FREE on the Facebook Marketplace section of the program. You can post about your services and connect with groups of people that need what you do. You can set up other accounts for free as well on Instagram and Twitter or other social connecting apps... any place that you can find to put out notifications that you are in business and available for clients. Letting people know you are selling or buying properties is only going to increase your exposure and start making a footprint for your business.

I personally love using social media because it allows me to advertise what my business is and what it offers to countless groups of people, individuals in my sphere of influence, and to other like-minded people who come across my page. The best part is it is FREE! I am all about the budget and spending what I need to not what I could. As your business grows, you can incorporate other strategies that require some budget consideration and financial obligations for marketing.

Join some local clubs of interest. Car clubs, garden clubs, or your child's school clubs where you are interacting with other people about life and it gives you an opportunity to share who you are and what you do. Make a point to attend the regular meetings and generate friendships with the people in these groups. Even if they don't need your services, they may know someone who does.

Marketing should become second nature to you in that you are always promoting yourself and your business. You should be proud of what you do and want to share it with the masses, find ways to get your name out to the public and set yourself apart from the other people who claim to do what you do.

If you have not already done so, go ahead and get started on setting everything up. Pick a name, set up a business entity, and order some business cards. Then once you get them, start handing them out. Start posting online that you are in business and be ready to talk to people. Just think if you touch 5 new potential clients a day 5 days a week to start; that is 100 new potential clients in 1 month. Those people know other people and before you know it, your name is out there and business will start to pick up and take off.

Don't be afraid to be a success. Fear is a liar and will try to stop you from answering calls, making offers, and talking to potential clients - don't let it stop you. You can do this and you can find the success you thought you could have.

Budgets, Banks, and Borrowing

Ahhh the B's of investing. Some of these terms can be kind of frightening, but once you understand how useful they are and how they can help you accelerate your business, you will learn to love them.

<u>Budgets</u>

Just like marketing, if you don't have a budget, you won't go very far. Every business needs to set a budget. There needs to be an overall business budget, a budget for marketing, a budget for acquiring the real estate, and a budget for what you plan to do with the investment once you acquire it. At the end of the day, it is all about the numbers.

Making a budget can be challenging because it is hard to foretell the future in some situations - such as rehab, but it is still a necessary part of the business. There are a lot of unseen things in properties that can go wrong but as a general rule, you can set up a budget very easy and operate efficiently within the numbers you set up. The golden rule of budget setting is once you set a budget, stick to it! If something unforeseen arises, do your best to stick as close as you can to it or before you know it, you will be upside down spending more than you are making.

Let's set up a basic budget scenario for acquiring a property, rehabbing it, and selling it with a realtor. Let's say you have access to $95,000.00 to do a deal and you find a fixer-upper house in a decent neighborhood and you are interested in buying it to flip and resell. The property is for sale for $50,000.00. There are other houses with similar physical parameters that have sold (not for sale- very important) for about $130,000.00. It seems like a decent spread financially, right?

After you walk the property with a contractor and get an idea of what needs to be done to get it to the $130,000.00 price point, you learn that it needs about $25,000.00 in renovations. Now you are in $75,000.00 without any unforeseen challenges. Once you list it, you can conservatively say that 7% will go towards closing and realtors commissions so that's about $9,100.00. Not to mention a reserve for rehab coverage and the closing costs when you purchased it.

When buying an investment property, you want to try to be all-in no more than 70% of its after repair value. So, for this example, with the 70% After Repair Value, you want to try to be all in no more than $91,000.00

When you run these numbers, here is what you see:

$130,000.00- resale price
- 9,100.00- closing and Realtor resell side(7%)
- $50,000.00- Purchase price
- $ 1,500.00- Buy side closing costs(3%)

- $25,000.00- Rehab
- $ 2,500.00- overages rehab
- <u>$ 3,000.00- Carry costs(insurance, utilities, lawn care...)</u>
$ 38,900.00- Projected profit if all goes as planned-

At the end of the day, this looks to be a good profit on this flip. If you set aside the taxes owed from this project right away, you still profit a pretty penny. If you go back and look at your budget of $95,000.00 on this property and all the expenses - which is called being "all-in", using this example, you are in about $91,100 which is right on budget and adheres to the 70% rule previously mentioned.

Since $38,900.00 is a solid profit and you may be comfortable with less. You can adjust the budget and splurged on cosmetic items and use a higher quality granite, fancy lights if you think you can get a better return... But before you do that, make sure you do not need to replace a roof expectantly or your budget can soar out of control.

Setting a preferred profit budget per transaction is a good idea. It gives you a baseline of what you feel is appropriate for you and your business needs. Keep in mind, however, every opportunity may not be a good deal and meet your budget or profit parameters so it is ok to pass if you have to push to make it work or you are compromising on your goals and budget outlines. There are way too many deals out there to force one to work.

Before we jump to banks, I want to share some ideas about running numbers for rehab. There are several ways to do this and most of them are very effective. If you are looking to do mass flips, it would be beneficial for you to set up a standard material list you use on every deal. Same paint colors, same cabinet style, same flooring, and carpet... This way, you have a solid gauge on numbers when you are walking a property. You can know that the type of flooring you are choosing will always be around $4.00 sq ft purchased and installed or that the light choices you use will be around $700.00 for the whole house. If you shop around for a set style of products and use the same vendors, you will get good deals and discounts for repeat spending and you can set a better budget. Also, using a setlist of materials makes turn over in your rentals so much easier - we will go over that later.

If you have never set up a rehab budget, however, learning how to assess a rehab and make a budget for a flip may seem like a daunting task when you are getting started to take a contractor with you and walk the property. Listen to what they think needs to be done and what they think things may cost for them to do the job. Markdown material items they point out and write down obvious ones you see as well. Do this with at least three different contractors because each one does it differently. They use different vendors for materials and get discounts from some places and not others - pick their brain and see what works for them. Then take some time to look up national averages for certain projects. Look up the national average for flooring, or how much should a painter charge per square foot to paint. Then look at your area and see if it's cheaper where you live or more expensive. Also, consider the investment you are looking at. Is it a higher valued property that required nicer finishes or is it a middle of the road rental where you can use builder grade?

If you search the internet for spreadsheets for budgets and tools to use to determine what percent of the budget goes to the kitchen or the bath, you will find lots of options and all have valid concepts. You need to take that information, take the averages for your area, and create your own budget outline that you can reuse on every property.

But if variety is your thing and you like to change it up on every property that is ok as well, just make sure you are being mindful of the location of the property, the values in the area so you do not overspend the neighborhood, and that you stay within your budget. Be mindful of the types of properties available in the area so that you are not offering something so unique, it will not appraise or have comparable sales to give you the value you want.

Be disciplined and you will find the profit you desired and got into real estate investing for.

Banks

Do not be afraid! Banks can be a great tool if you know what banks to use and why to use them.

When looking for a Bank to do business with, you need to assess all they offer for a small business. Big banks do not always give small businesses breaks in account balances or discounts on wire fees, so you need to look around.

Credit unions are typically easier to work with in regards to flexible terms for the independent business owner and small business. Even better is a small hometown credit union that typically has 3 branches or less. They want the community business and offer incentives for new accounts, business owners, and the small business itself.

When calling around to find an institution that is right for you, there are some initial questions you might want to ask to see if they really are a good fit.

1) Do they work with investors?
2) Will they work with an investor that does not live locally or if the property is not local. (maybe you want to expand your footprint someday)
3) Are there certain counties or cities they will or will not work in?
4) What incentives do they offer business owners? If you are a veteran business owner, ask about incentives about that as well.
5) What is the requirement for monthly account balances and are there fees for going under that?

6) How long will they hold funds wired or deposited? Is there an amount threshold for that "holding" requirement?

As you converse with the bank, you may add or remove questions or expand on them. As long as they will meet your needs as an investor, that is what is most important.

Opening a business account is just as easy as a personal account. You will need to bring your ID, business documents, and an EIN number (Employer Identification Number). You get an EIN number from IRS.gov site - it is free and gives you the ability to open a bank account and pay employees along the way. Get a Debit card and some checks. You will want to buy all marketing times and rehab materials with the debit card and always, did I say ALWAYS, pay your contractors and service providers with a business check for accounting purposes and ease of banking verification for accounting.

Use your bank incentives and get to know the tellers and branch managers. This will help you build rapport for future needs such as borrowing. It also lends to other potential opportunities such as referrals to other bank customers looking to invest. If the bank has to foreclose on a property, they may call and offer it to you and with every relationship. There comes a time where you may get approved for something because of your relationship at that particular branch that you may not have had the opportunity for at a different location where the person does not know you.

Borrowing

Borrowing funds for investing is a standard part of the industry. Paying cash is ideal but lending against or refinancing the investment to get the cashback keeps the wheel rolling.

Let's look at a few borrowing scenarios.

Private Lending - Private lending is borrowing funds from a private individual or entity for an agreed-upon return. Such as Uncle Joe, or Grandma Bette, or even someone's IRA account. This can be based on a personal relationship, the asset, or a combination of both. Also, this may or may not be recorded against the investment and is determined between you and the lender.

Private lending is lent with an interest amount in addition to the funds lent. If you borrow $100,000.00 at 10% interest, you will pay back $110,000.00 to the lender. The terms of this type of borrowing can be varied for the deal and amount of money lent. Private money can be lent for 30 days, 90 days, or a year whatever the parties agree to. You can make monthly interest payments and a balloon payment back at the end of the term, you can make monthly payments for the entire balance, or you can make one lump sum payment at the end of the term - for example, when the investment is flipped and sold.

Hard Money Lending - one of the most common forms of borrowing for newer investors because it is easier to get and is generally based on the asset you are borrowing against. Hard money requires "points plus interest". Points meaning a percentage of the loan amount PLUS the agreed-upon interest rate. For example, on a $100,000.00 hard money loan, you may have 2 points and 10%. Meaning you will pay $2,000.00 plus $10,000.00 in interest. Terms again agreed upon by the parties but the option to pay it all at the end is removed. Hard money is lent for the term of the project. If you are flipping, the loan must be paid back upon selling or refinancing the investment. The points charged in a hard money loan are paid upfront at the beginning of the loan and monthly interest payments with a balloon at the end of the term. Hard money loans are often recorded as a lien against the investment as well.

Bank Lending - Traditional lending with a bank is more detailed and requires personal and/or business records to validate the ability to pay back the loan. You will need to provide tax returns, pay stubs, profit, and loss statements for other investments and often carries a personal guarantee along with a business backing of the loan and the bank will look at your credit score and history.

Bank lending has an annual percentage rate charged against the loan amount and is paid monthly. Bank lending is a longer term with lower interest rates and is recorded against the investment. So, on a $100,000.00 loan, you may pay 6% interest annually over 15 years and you make a monthly payment until the loan is paid off.

Bank lending does have restrictions on the number of loans they can perform for one entity or person regulated by Freddy and Fanny UNLESS, and this is very important unless, they are a portfolio lending institution which means they keep all loans in house, service them internally, and do not report them. This is the best kind of lending because you can have many loans out at one time, and if you are a landlord who refinances rental, this could be a benefit.

Refinancing - Once you purchase an investment property and you decide to keep it as a rental, you can refinance it and pull out most of the money put in with a manageable mortgage that the tenant would cover through their monthly rental amount plus give you a small profit. This is called a cash-out refinance. Many banks will offer this type of lending but the banks you want to use are the portfolio lending institutions. They will, oftentimes, lend up 80% of the appraised value which should pull out all the funds you have in plus a little so you can move on to the next deal.

When looking for a cash-out refinance, you want to ask a few more questions of the lending institution:

> 1) What is the seasoning? Meaning how long do you have to own the property before they will refinance. You want to find a no-seasoning institution that looks at the fact

that the project is completed and that you have a tenant secured or that it is being marketed for a tenant. You will need to clarify this as this varies from lender to lender.

2) Is there a pre-payment penalty if you pay off the loan sooner than the maturity date?
3) If they are a portfolio lender, what are the lending limits for each entity borrowing? Is a dollar value or an amount of investments?
4) How quickly can they close on refinance?
5) What will they need per property to consider it for a cash-out refinance?

One of the great things here is that once you build a basic refinance relationship, you can expand into a purchase and rehab lending scenario with this same lender to buy and renovate properties which they can roll over from a rehab loan to a general loan once its rented and generating cash flow.

<u>Retirement Funds</u> - Using retirement funds are a great way to build your retirement virtually tax-free. Using your IRA, you can borrow funds, buy an investment, and the proceeds go back into your IRA account tax-free. Depending on the type of IRA you have, you may have to pay taxes to borrow upfront, but on a self-directed IRA, that money is paid when you transfer money out of a traditional IRA to the Self- Directed IRA. Then you can borrow without any further penalty. But again, app proceeds must go back into the IRA.

You can use someone else's retirements funds as well to do deals. This is a great way to borrow money but paying back the IRA your initial investment and any interest agreed to at the end of the investment term. IRA holders love to make money tax-free and will often lend purchase price and rehab amounts for the investment as long as they get all their funds plus interest back. So you are flipping an investment, making a profit, and using none of your own money.

There are several other very creative ways to borrow funds and each one can be as unique as the project you are using it on. Feel free to be creative with avenues and don't be afraid to think outside the box when using funds to do a deal. Just make sure you read the contracts, understand what is expected of you in return for using the money, and what the terms are for repayment.

Home Equity Line of Credit or HELOC

A HELOC is a form of lending that allows you to borrow against the equity you already have in a property. This type of borrowing requires you to submit personal documents to the Banks as well as having the property appraised to evaluate how much you can borrow. For example, if you own a house-personal or investment - that appraises $200,000.00 and you have a loan or mortgage on it for $110,000.00, there is $90,000.00 in equity. Each lending institution offers a different percentage of the open equity for a loan, so you will need to ask that question. So out of $90,000.00 in equity, you may get $75,000.00 - it is up to the lender's terms. That being said, $75,000.00 is a great lump of cash to use for purchase, rehab, or partnership. Each month, you make a payment on the HELOC which lowers the amount out on the loan, so each month, your payments may be less and less since you have less equity pulled out on the property. A HELOC can be used on anything really, but if you decide to go forward with a HELOC, then use the funds for something that will benefit your retirement or cash flow long term.

Line of Credit

The standard line of credit comes in 2 forms - Secured and Unsecured.

A Secured line of credit is a loan you get approved for and the lender uses something as collateral against the funds borrowed. Collateral depends on how much you want to borrow. That way if you happen to default on the loan, the bank can seize the asset for repayment. An Unsecured Line of Credit is where the Bank feels you hold enough merit based on your financials to repay the loan and you are personally guaranteeing you will pay it back. Your signature is golden and means that you promise to pay the loan back no matter what.

Both of these methods require a qualification from the lending institution that you choose and they will look at financials, credit score, debt to income, assets if needed… again up to the lender's requirements.

When calling a credit union regarding LOC options, here is an outline you can follow.

When you call each credit union and ask to speak to someone about a line of credit. When that person answers the phone, just restate that you have some questions about their lines of credit, then ask the following questions:

Note: DO not allow them to say, "Send me your financials or SSN# first, then we can talk." If they do respond by saying, "I would like to ask you a few questions first to see if there is a good fit."

- What will you use (real estate/car/etc) as collateral for a line of credit?
- What is your loan to value for a LOC?
- What criteria do they base their decision on?
- Are their lines of credit reported to the credit bureaus?
- What is their current interest rate for the lines of credit?
- How long does it take to approve an application for a line of credit?
- After 12 months, would the LOC be reviewed and be eligible to be increased if everything went perfect?
- Do you have anything else I should know about your lines of credit product offering?

Then thank them for their time and let them know we will be back in touch with them.

Then take the information and you have to think about the program, compare it to other lenders, and see what best works for you.

No Money Investing

Investing with no personal capital is something many have heard of but not many understand how to generate cash flow using other people's money. You can join in with someone on any type of investing noted earlier in this book or ones that you discover on your own. No two deals are exactly the same, and therefore, can be crafted in its own uniqueness.

There is nothing saying you need to be wealthy to invest in real estate. There are no rules about where to get the funds to buy or renovate properties and there is nothing saying that you need to do any deal as a private business entity. Consider partnering with other investors who have the capital to spend but do not have the time or know-how to buy or renovate. Joint ventures and partnerships are a great alternative for both sides.

There are many individuals who are cash-rich but

have no knowledge or time to do the research needed to purchase an investment, do not have the time to coordinate contractors or manage a renovation on an investment, and they regularly look for individuals who have the knowledge and time to do just that and are willing to give up a portion of the cash flow for that time and effort. Part of the cash flow is better than no cash flow at all.

Who are these people with cash looking to invest and where can you find them? They are everywhere and you likely talk to them on a daily basis. You will find them at doctor's offices, dentist offices, law offices, mill workers, your retired neighbor next door, or even your great aunt... yes, we are talking about Doctors, Dentists, Lawyers, people who work long hours and irregular schedules or people who simply have managed their earnings well but don't know where to begin. Often these individuals want to invest and buildup their retirement but simply lack the time or knowledge.

Locating these partners usually comes from unconventional marketing and using word of mouth recommendations. You will need to change up and advance your marketing techniques by attending events where these individuals may come together for leisure time. Events such as business after hours, cigar bars, country clubs, community events, and certainly using their professional services for daily life are all great ways to come face to face with these partners. These are individuals who would be good to give business cards to and set up a follow-up meeting on a lunch break to discuss how the two of you can work together and how you can help use their funds to help them and you bring added cash flow.

Partnering requires a more mature level of communication and confidence that you know what you are doing and that you can indeed offer something to them of value. These individuals often scrutinize things a little closer than the average investor. They prefer to know as many facts as they can and analyze the information before making the decisions to actually move forward. Once they gather the information needed, they will expect a contract or written agreement to line out the details of the partnership and how the cash flow will flow in and how it will be divided between the parties. You can have a joint venture agreement or partnership agreement drafted by a local attorney or use one that another investor doing partnerships may be using. It is important to make sure that both parties agree to the terms and sign the agreement before the transaction ensues. Once the investment comes through and cash flow is generated, a good accounting system needs to be used so that at any time an accurate account of the finances can be shared and viewed by all parties. In the end, investment funds are disseminated according to the agreement and parties go their respective ways.

Using other people's money also works in ways we discussed in the borrowing section of this book and you learned you can use funds from other sources to buy, renovate, and generate cash flow in many ways.

All of this can work for the good of all parties. In cases where the projects may not go as planned or a deal goes over budget, there can be challenges that need to be considered. When other people funds are used, it is imperative that those funds are replaced before anyone even considers taking a profit. You want to ensure that those with the funds are made as whole as possible so even if the profit is much less or non-existent, their initial investment is returned to them. This is the most ethical way to ensure that your reputation and ability to do right by your funding sources are foremost in the contractual agreement.

Types of Investing

This chapter alone could be an entire book because real estate has so many avenues and each investor has their own ideas of what they want to buy and how they want to make money so think outside the box and see what works for you. We will focus on just a few types of investing that the majority of Investors use to generate cash flow on a regular and monthly basis.

Wholesaling

You may say, "Really, for cash flow?" I say YES! If you operate a consistent wholesale investment business, then cash flow comes monthly, weekly, or even a couple of times a week.

Let's look at what wholesaling really is. This is the act of securing a piece of real estate with a legal and binding purchase agreement. Then you can do

1 of 2 things.

   1) Assign the contract to an end buyer for a small fee.

OR

   2) You can do what is called a double close or a simultaneous close. This is you buying the property in full then selling it to an end buyer, the same day typically, for a slightly larger profit. Both of these require you to do no physical work to the house or make any improvements.

One of the most important things to remember in an assignment of contract is that you do not have a legal right to sell the property, but you have a legal right to sell your contract to buy the property. So, be careful not to relist or market the property once you have it under contract unless your contract allows for that and be honest if you are assigning it.

What is a good fee to charge on an assignment of a contract? This is a personal choice but I would say no more than $5,000.00 on an average priced property. Now, you're not going to charge $5000.00

on a property that is being bought and sold for around $15,000.00 that would be taking advantage. Be reasonable with your fee and make it appropriate to the purchase price of the house. The reason we suggest a lower on an assignment fee amount is that at the end of the day, you are not fulfilling the whole obligation of the contract. You are assigning your rights to someone else to fulfill it and asking for a small fee for your time and effort in locating and securing the property under contract. Also when assigning, you need to have full disclosure to the person you are assigning the contract to. After all, they are accepting the contract you wrote and agreeing to fulfill it.

When offing the contract to your end buyer, make sure you send them a copy of the purchase agreement you negotiated along with your assignment of the contract document, so they can see fully what it is they are agreeing to purchase and the terms they will need to adhere to.

A double close or simultaneous close is a more

involved and detailed process. This involves you securing the property under contract, physically purchasing the property through the agreed-upon closing method, then reselling the property, typically the same day, to another buyer for a larger markup on the selling price.

What this means is you can find a distressed property at a great price. Once you have assessed it and run the projected numbers, you have determined that you go this property at 0.20 on the dollar. You have an end buyer who will pay 0.30 on the dollar, so you can resell this property to them for the difference. So, if you buy a $150,000.00 house for $30,000.00 (which is .20 on the dollar) and your buyer will pay 0.30 cents, you can resell it to them for $45,000.00. So, you bought it for $30,000.00, resold it the same day for $45,000.00, and you make $15,000.00 in this example.

This type of transaction does not require you to share your purchase agreement or details with the end buyer because you are fulfilling your agreement with the initial seller which is a private agreement between you and the person you are buying it from. Your contract with your end buyer can have your own terms. You will draft a separate purchase agreement with your end buyer because, even if it is just for an hour, you will be the legal owner of the property and can sell it under whatever terms your end buyer agree to.

Both of these are a repeatable process and you can do multiple properties like this at a time since you are not actually going to need funds to rehab the investment, or in some cases of the assignment, you won't even need funds to close on the sale. You can even adjust the amount you make per deal to meet the goals you have set. I would caution you that making a good deal for your end buyer keeps them coming back, so be fair. This keeps bringing you cash flow and a lively hood to meet your goals on an ongoing basis. If you take too much of the spread on a deal and your end buyer has to push to make the numbers work on their end, they may not buy from you again because the deal was not as profitable in the end as they had hoped.

Fix and Flips

Buying a property to fix and flip for retail can be a very lucrative adventure or can drain your bank account. This type of investing requires a more detailed look at the numbers, what rehab needs to be done to make sure the resale value appraises and meets market standards and at the end of the project, there is profit to be made. This can be a good source of cash flow if you keep the rehabs ongoing and start one as soon as you complete one. You can use the funds generated in one transaction to live on and partially or totally fund the next deal.

You will need to consider your finances with this type of investment as well. If you need to finance any portion of it and have to repay that with interest or points added, you need to ensure that the profit margin can cover everything and still put money back in your pocket.

All that being said, I think this can also be the most

fun line of real estate investing. It allows the creative side of the investing to come forward and you can take a house that has been neglected and un-updated and turn it into a place for someone to call home.

We talked about budgets earlier and setting a budget here is very important. You should try to get all the rehab estimates in before you close on the investment so that you are clear on what is needed and going to be done and how much you anticipate spending. This will help you create a clear snapshot of the overall project, how much you can expect to pay out on the rehab, and how much you potentially could make on the transaction once it resells.

When assessing a fix and flip, you need to make sure that either you or a seasoned contractor assess the property as early as on the buying stage as possible. We suggest you do this during your inspection timeframe in accordance with the purchase agreement. This window of time allows you inspect the property and get a good estimate on the rehab needed, and if it appears to be too much, you can cancel the purchase agreement based upon the inspection and amount of rehab being greater than anticipated.

If during this timeframe you determine that the investment still meets good parameters and you decide to move forward, you should still be diligent to get as much information on the renovation as you can before closing the deal. Set a day and have several contractors meet you at the project and get estimates together, outline materials needed, timeframes, and costs so that once the transaction closes, you can begin to renovate right away and not get too far along in the timeframe with nothing happening.

Once the transaction closes, demolition should begin the same day or within 24 hours. Depending on how much demolition there is will determine the next phases beginning date. A demo should be outlined and your crew should understand exactly what needs to come out so that you are not removing things once the repairs have begun.

Next is prep work, patching holes, and electric and plumbing upgrades or repairs. This stage is the foundation of how the end product will look. If the prep work is poor, your end product will look poor and yield you less of a profit. If you or your crew take a little extra time to ensure that the walls are smooth with no nail holes or blemishes, the new paint will go on smooth and give a good clean appearance. If the subfloor is uneven or weak in spots, the new flooring will not lay properly and there may be gaps or bumps in the floor. You want the new flooring or carpet to lay flat on the surface so that it does not create a tripping hazard or that nothing falls through the floor once furnishing is placed on it.

The next steps are cosmetic. Paint, cabinets, light fixtures, flooring, doors, or whatever you put on your scope of work. I would recommend doing a walk through after each task is completed because some of them depend on the next stage, and if it is not right at initial install, the next step will be incorrect as well.

Once each contractor is completed with their task, walk the job with them and sign off on it with them. This ensures that you have verified the job is done and initiates final payment. DO NOT pay a contractor if you have not seen the completed product. This also allows you to test the job to ensure it works. Such as Electric - do the lights turn on and off, does the ceiling fan work, or do the 3-way switches function properly? Also plumbing - does the water heater work and does hot water actually flow from the faucets, do the drain lines drain efficiently, and do the shower heads turn on without leaks? All these things can be called out in a home inspection and cause delays and more money. This also allows you to have the contractor fix any issues right there rather than calling them back out at the end of the job to make a repair once they have already been paid in full.

Once the job is completed you should do a whole

house walk-through and do a blue tape day. A blue tape day is when you take blue painters and put a piece of tape on all the things that are not done or not done to your expectations. This gives the contracting team a room by room punch list of detailed items to fix before the house is signed off on and goes up for sale.

Once the blue tape items are completed sign off on the jobs and paid your team, now it is time to get it sold. You can sell it yourself or list it with a Realtor - it is your preference. Just make sure that if you choose the realtor route, like the example earlier, you account for listing and realtor fees.

After it is up for sale, make sure you have someone tending to lawn maintenance or winter snow shoveling so the curb appeal stays at its best. Once you have an offer, set up closing and collect your cash flow in this transaction and get going on the next one.

Rentals also known as Buy and Holds

Buying properties to keep as rentals give you long-term cash flow. This is something that generates money every month for as long as you own the investment.

Buying a rental can be slightly different than a flip in that you may not put high-quality materials in a rental or you may decide to buy it already rented and make upgrades along the way.

Assessing what a rental can generate each month requires you to look around the area and see what other rentals are going for and what the condition of those homes are to warrant the money generated each month. You can find information about rental rates on line pretty easy or you can coordinate with a property manager to see what properties are renting for in that area. Then you can determine what level of rehab to do or if maybe it just needs new paint.

I might suggest buying a vacant home, fixing it up,

and using it as a rental. I suggest this because by doing this, you get to control the quality of investment and you know what the true condition is before someone lives in it. If you do more than one rental you can use the same materials, paint color, and flooring in each investment because this allows you to control cost going in by buying in bulk and it allows you to control recovery when a tenant moves out by doing touch up paint rather than whole house painting. All this controls the flow of cash in and out of the investment. By buying vacant rehabbing and then renting, you also control the condition if you choose to use a property manager.

Using a property manager can be a tough decision. It seems like it may be easier to just manage it yourself, and at times, that may be ok. When your rental investment portfolio increases, it may be more difficult to manage many properties and keep up with maintenance repairs, move in and move out inspections, and paperwork. So considering using a property manager may be a good idea. A Property Manager will take care of qualifying tenants, doing move and move out inspections, collecting the rent, fielding and managing repair calls-even at 2 am, they have crews to do the work needed when someone moves out, and if needed, they can and will coordinate eviction proceedings if you have a tenant that, in the end, does not pay. If you look at it this way, it may help. I would rather pay someone 10% of my profit to do 100% of the work and collect 90% of the profit doing nothing. So using a Property Manager may make cash flow margins increase in the long run.

The big benefit to rental properties is that you get a monthly check for rent that covers taxes, insurance, and some unforeseen maintenance calls and can still generate a profit for you. Having more than one rental increases that cash flow and having a rental portfolio generates cash flow on an ongoing basis.

Multi-family
Similar to the above rental option in regards to generating monthly cash flow, the multi-family unit increases that cash flow exponentially. However, the

likelihood that you acquire a multi-family unit empty may not be possible and you may already have the cashflow to make repairs as units come vacant.

Multi-family can be a large building with many units or many building with units such as an apartment complex. Or it can be several smaller properties with 2-4 units in each. The combination is endless but the concept is the same.

Buying multi-family does require different diligence criteria. You need to look at the numbers as a whole. How many vacancies, what is the monthly maintenance, what utilities does the owner cover, are the units at market rent, what is needed to improve the property to raise the rents? The overall renovation numbers on multi-units are greater only because of total square footage but the per-unit cost should be smaller since, typically, apartments are not over 1000 sqft per unit. In the big picture, the rental return numbers can be greater as well once the units and property are updated and rented at market rents. Not to mention managed properly also increases the cash flow opportunity. So using a property manager for these types of investments is a given - trying to manage a large multi-unit internally would inhibit you from growing in other areas so don't skimp on this piece of the investment.

Trailer Parks or Manufactured Home Communities
Quickly becoming a thing of the past, the Mobile Home Community is the secret to the real estate ATM machine.

Most parks or communities are family-owned and the upcoming generation is not so excited about managing the family trailer park, so as the owners retire, they are selling off the parks at a premium.

Parks are owned and managed a couple of different ways to generate cash flow.

Park-Owned Trailers vs. resident-owned Trailers

Park-owned trailers are just that. The park owns the trailers and rents them out to tenants for cash flow. This is similar to a typical rental in that the park is then responsible for maintenance on the trailer, the park grounds, and typically, the utilities. Along with the trailer rent, the tenant also pays a lot. So even though there is income, there is also an outgo for maintenance.

Resident-owned trailer parks are the golden ATM. The residence owns and maintains their own trailers, pay their own utilities, and mow and maintain the grounds around their homes. The park owner collects lot rent and only has to pay for landscaping for general areas and basic utilities for the office and street lights in the park. The cash flow coming in can be much more lucrative since there is really no expense for maintenance or upkeep on any physical units; you just collect money on the land the trailers sit on.

It is easier to manage a small to medium park internally because of the limited maintenance, but if it happens to be a larger park and you have other investments as well, you should consider using a property manager. Most parks use someone who lives in the park for management or someone that is on-site during normal business hours to manage vacant home sales and coordinate the landscaping and grounds maintenance duties. You may consider using a management couple to live on-site and offer free lot rent in exchange for work in the park.

By the owner not managing the property, it also sets apart the owner from daily decision-making for delinquent residence. When tough decisions need to be made, the owner can make them free of the input and complaining of the residence because they don't like the decision. Or if you should ever need to evict someone, your manager handles all that, and when the judge asks if your manager wants to make exceptions, they can answer within the parameters of their job decision-making.

Separating yourself from management on real estate investments is generally a good thing. You can focus more on working ON your business rather than IN your business.

Commercial

Commercial Real Estate Investing is a breed all its own. This is where you are buying strip malls, shopping centers, or large areas of land for development. While the development is not necessarily a cash flow option, it can pay off big in the end.

For this book, let's consider strip malls. Do you know the long buildings along busy roads that have take-out food locations, nail salons, laundromats, or cellphone stores? They are a one-stop-shop in some cases. Owning one of these doesn't always carry the maintenance and upkeep as a single-family rental does but the building is larger and repairs can add up faster than you think. The tenants are typically not as rough on the building as they are not living there day in and day out and the internal activity is not as damaging.

In a well-maintained building, you can rent or lease out each space to a specific business for a determined length of time. They are signing multiple-year leases expecting to generate the level of business needed to grow.

Lease amounts are determined on a per square foot price. That square foot price is determined on the desirability and location of the building. A strip mall on a road that is considered a secondary road would not charge as much like a strip mall that was located right of a freeway exit which is a location that a lot of travelers drive by and need those services.

Let's say that you own a strip mall that is 15,000 sqft and the going rate for your high traffic area is $2.50 per sq. ft. That's an estimated $37,000.00 a month in lease income. Sounds great! Then you need to consider that your lease with the tenant probably includes you paying utilities and offers parking lot and sidewalk maintenance which all come out of the monthly lease income. You also need to carry a higher level of insurance since hundreds of people will be frequenting the strip mall. If someone gets hurt or something happens to them while on your property, that can cost your insurance a lot and maybe you if you are not covered properly. And you need to set money aside for taxes which, as a commercial business owner, you should pay quarterly. After all those deductions, you find that your cash flow every month may only be $8,000.00 which is still good and nothing to shake a stick. Commercial properties just require a higher level of funds to enter in to and a higher level of funds to operate. If you have many commercial spaces, your overall cash flow can replace any smaller investment cash flow very easily.

Commercial investing can be highly profitable and investing at this typically comes with time. You will need to get some experience under your belt and a solid understanding of how to manage funds, manage budgets and manage large leases. It is all possible and anyone can jump into the commercial sector. It just requires some seasoning as an investor.

Turn-Key Cash Flow

Turn-Key cash flow requires a bit more effort but the cash flow that can be generated from it can be very satisfying.

Turn-Key Investing is a combination of a couple of the above options but with a twist. You are doing the investing for a 3rd party. If you offer to wholesale and rehabbing for a flip or to hold as a rental for a 3rd party, you can generate cash flow in more than one avenue.

To begin this form of cash flow, I suggest that you have some deals under your best and are comfortable with the buying, flipping, selling, and renting portion of the business because it will require you to offer a full set of services to another investor who typically lives outside the area but wants to grow their real estate portfolio or generate their own cash flow but the market they are in does not allow them to capitalize on that.

This is different than any of the lending options we touched on earlier in that the funds used are the investors for their own investment and you are creating cash flow by offering the systems and managing the process for them time and time again. The only similar process is either the wholesale or double close part of the transaction.

Initially, you want to already have a pool of investment buyers looking in your geographic areas of investing. You can build a buyer's list using any form of marketing that lets out-of-state investors know that your area has great purchase prices, great returns and that you have the system needed to ensure the project goes from beginning to end and they don't need to come here at all. Building this relationship may take some time because the likelihood of some total stranger giving money to you to do a project without knowing you will take some trust-building. You will need to reassure them of your past efforts of finding great investments, conducting successful rehab projects, managing a budget, and your use of reliable service providers already at your disposal. You will also need to ensure that you use legal means to buy close and transact the process; meaning you need to use an attorney or a title company to buy and sell the property.

Overall you need a good portfolio set up of who you are and the investments you have completed and can show you have generated the positive cash flow you can start marketing yourself.

Once you have a specific buyer relationship confirmed, begin to personally shop for them in regards to what they want in an investment. It's easier to find what they want rather than finding something and hoping they want to buy it from you. So during the relationship-building process, spend time getting to know your buyer. Ask them what they want and what you can find for them. I have included a basic worksheet that you can use and modify to suit your needs as you grow to help you gather as much information as you can about what your buyer wants so it makes it easier to match up a potential investment with a buyer in your client list.

Below is a list of questions you can use to "qualify" a CASH buyer:

Buyer Name/Company Name:
_____

Phone: _____
Email: _____

1. What areas are you most interested in

buying?

_____

_____

2. What type of properties do you want to purchase? SFR/Commercial/Multi-Family

_____

_____

3. How many beds/baths/sq.ft./etc.

_____

_____

4. What level of rehab are you comfortable with? (Heavy-structural, medium-remove a wall, light-cosmetic)

_____

_____

5. What is your maximum purchase price or ALL-

IN number including rehab and fees?

_____

_____

6. How much profit would you like to make from each deal?

_____

_____

7. Are you looking to Flip or Hold rentals? If rental, will you want to cash out Refinance?

_____

_____

8. How quickly can you close?

_____

_____

Using a basic form helps you get to know your buyer will show them that you are interested in what they want and not just what you can find for them.

Once you gather this information, you can begin to look and market for an investment that meets their criteria. Once you have found a potential candidate, you need to present the purchase portion of it just as if you were wholesaling or doing a simultaneous close. The only caveat here is that you need to include the Turn-Key piece of the transaction. You will generate cash flow from the initial sale to your end buyer but now you can offer a 2nd and or 3rd piece to them.

The 2nd piece is offering to manage the renovation for them and the 3rd is offering to help them manage it as a rental or you can help them find a realtor to sell it after it is done and ready for retail sale.

Before presenting the deal, you should already know if your client wants to keep it as a rental or flip it. Rehab can be slightly different for a rental as opposed to a flip because the finished are typically not expensive. Therefore, your rehab numbers may vary and knowing what the plan is will be a big help.

You should not only offer the deal as a purchase, but you also need to offer the deal with all the information needed regarding the rehab, your fee to do the rehab, what the market rent for the property would be, or what the after repair value is based on comparable sold properties in the area. These are not numbers you guess at or just look online - you would hate to present misinformation that would cost your client to generate less or lose money because you would lose them as a client.

To offer the rehab management portion of the transaction, you need to have done some more detailed research on what the rehab will actually cost and what you can get it done for. This information will take talking to contractors and getting bids, resourcing realtors and property managers in that area, and if possible, getting hard data to present to your client showing the results of what you are saying the values are. In wholesaling or simultaneous closings, you are giving a good ball-park estimate of what rehab could be, but here you are going to be responsible for actually doing the rehab, managing the budget, and making sure the investment goes through with the numbers you have proposed.

Once you have collected all the data and have your numbers ready to go, you need to determine what to charge for your management fee on the renovation coordination. Keep in mind the management fee needs to be included as part of the overall numbers and they still have been in your client's all-in range. Your fee needs to justify the work but keep in mind you are also profiting on the wholesale portion of the deal as well so don't go crazy and overcharge your client. If you are not a general contractor and are just coordinating the rehab, your fee is less and spate. If you are a general contractor, then you will get paid as part of the rehab and should not be a separate line item to charge your client.

It is helpful to send over a spreadsheet or detailed

outline of the entire investment along with photos and any data you have collected about rental income or retail sales values as well. You can just send one number for the entire rehab unless your client wants it broken down. But remember, you will be the one your client gives the rehab funds to, you will be the one buying materials if needed and paying the contractors so unless you work it out where your client pays everyone individually and buys materials remotely, you don't need to break it down to the penny. I would, however, separate out your management fee so they see that you are being compensated for your time in that role.

The 3rd area is coordinating the rental or the resale of the property. If you are a licensed realtor, you will not ask for any fee outside your realtor commission for listing and selling the property - that goes against realtor protocol in almost every state. You may ask for a referral fee if you find them a good realtor that sells the house but taking an added fee before the person you referred is not very professional. If you are a licensed property manager, again, you will not take an added fee for taking on the management other than your standard fees. If you are privately finding them a tenant and your client wants to manage it themselves, then it is appropriate to take a finder's fee for obtaining a qualified tenant. If your client asks you to manage the property for them but you are not licensed, you need to see what the laws are for that in your area. But in most areas, if you are not advertising a property management service and privately managing a property for someone you do not need a license. In this case, you can work out whatever fee schedule is appropriate for the management in your area.

A presentation could look something like this:

123 Main St Anytown, USA 98765
ARV(After Repair Value) $ 151,000.00

| Purchase price | $70,000.00(this includes your wholesale or simultaneous close profit) |

Rehab Estimate $25,000.00
<u>Rehab Management $ 5,000.00</u>
All-IN $100,000.00

Sold Comparable values are as follows:

487 South St sold for $155,000.00
258 North Woods sold for $147,000.00
957 Backlot St sold for $157,000.00
357 Estate Dr sold for $145,000.00

All sold comparables are located within 0.75 miles of 123 Main St. and sold within the last 6 months.

Estimated rental rates in the area for a 3 bed/1.5 bath 1200sqft home are between $950.00-$1,200.00 a month, so I would estimate $1,050.00 a month.

(You generally want to offer the lower value so that just in case a renter cannot be found and a price adjustment is needed your client can at least know the low end to expect. Under promise and over deliver – always makes you look good and makes your client happy).

Estimated completion time for renovation is 4 weeks from the date of close.

Add the photos and the comparable data and ask your client to replay within 72 hours. This way, if for some reason they pass on the deal, you still have time to offer it to another client or get out of the deal.

Once they replay with a yes, draft the sell side of the contracts and get them sent to the title for closing. You will need a separate contract for the management of the rehab - this does not need to be sent to the title company. This agreement is between the parties only. The rehab management agreement should outline the scope of work, timeframe to completion, how the funds will be sent to you, and how you will report back to your client on the progress of the renovation project. The disbursement of funds is totally up to you and your client but breaking up the payout into 2 or 3 payments is generally good practice. Typically half up front, 25% in the middle, and the final 25% when rehab is about a week before the project is done. Separating out your management fee should be part of that agreement - half up front and a half when you are 100% completed. Renovation updates generally occur on a weekly basis with an outline of the funds spent and photos of the progress. This way they can feel confident that you are doing what you promised and are contracted to do and gives you more credibility.

When the project is about 1 week away from being completed, you can send for final payments along with an initiation to the final process of renting or selling the investment. If you are coordinating this process, you need a 3rd agreement for whatever your compensation is. If it is a finder's fee for a realtor referral and the house sells, outline that fee in an agreement. If there is to be an agreement for you to manage the rental, then this needs to be contracted as well. It may seem like there are a lot of contracts, but keep in mind, each action you perform is separate from the previous and having a contract offers a sense of responsibility to perform and compensate. If you do deals with verbal agreements or email agreements, they may or may not stand up in court since all the details are not spelled out and it leaves room for misinterpretation. A good contract makes a good working relationship. Always use a contract!

Once the project is completed and you have finished your responsibility, you can begin to coordinate your next project. I would encourage you to keep the pipeline open so that you are marketing and researching the next deal before the current deal is completed. This keeps your cash flow coming in on a regular basis. This is also a good reason to have more than 1 investor client so that you can move from one to next. In case it takes longer for the investment to sell or get rented, you are not stuck waiting for that same investor to buy your next deal.

How to Locate Properties for Cash Flow

Now that we have covered all the upfront on how to get information, we can go over locating these amazing investment opportunities that are going to bring you the cash flow we have been talking about.

There are endless ways to find properties and you can certainly create more to fit your business model and your personality so enjoy the hunt for great deals.

Since you should already have your business entity set up and business cards at least ordered, you can begin to market for properties. Slightly different than marketing just your business, this is going to appeal to a certain group of people who need or want to sell their property.

Consider what type of real estate you are starting to focus on. Single-family homes are the most common, the most readily available and the most economical for getting started in real estate investing. The single-family residences or SFRs that you want to look for are houses that you can buy under market value. These houses have work to be done on them, have been vacant for a while, are un-kept rentals that landlords no longer want, estate properties that the family doesn't want to keep, or just that the current owner simply cannot afford to keep up. The reasons are ongoing but the bottom line is - it is a distressed property because the owner is unable to keep it or wants to keep it.

So much money has been spent trying to figure out ways to get the attention of the property owner who just doesn't want the house any longer but the truth is if you just get your information in front of them someway somehow and then responding when they reach out, you will see this is the most successful way. A lot of newer investors are so excited to get going and they put out marketing to get properties, but then when the seller calls, they don't answer because they don't know what to say or how to move on to the next level. We are going to go over just a few ways to get in front of sellers and when they do call, we will go over what to ask them and how to assess the property to see if it will be a good cash flow option.

Of course, you have or will have business cards you can set out or hand out and there are many ways to freely advertise that you buy distressed properties - but let's think bigger than that. Let's look at options that may cost you some money, but if you can do just 1 deal from it, you will have paid for the marketing.

Direct Mail

Direct Mail is sending out mailers directly to property owners who have a certain set of criteria you want to target. These criteria may make this group of people more motivated to want to sell. You can create mailing lists yourself from public records looking for out of state owners, landlords who have less than 5 properties (less than 5 because they likely manage them internally and are dealing with turnovers, maintenance calls, missed rent payments, and just are tired of the game) or even houses that have a lot of equity and the owner has lived there for over 20 years. The other option is you can go online to one of the many direct mail companies and set up an account and create a list through them.

Creating a criteria list is easy to do because the sites give you click options to choose from and you can see how many potential sellers you will mail to before you even go to the next step. Highly motivated sellers are generally out of town owners who have had the property for more than 5 years and own it free and clear. You can add other criteria like a percentage of equity value, occupied or vacant status, pending foreclosure, or bank-owned homes. See what combination meets your spending limits and generate a list. Often you can download that list for future use as well or do a mailing campaign on your own.

Most online direct marketing sites allow you the option to create a mailer, postcard, or letter to send out and they will generate it and mail it out for you. Some even track the returned mail notices so you don't mail to the dead lead again and waste money. Once the mailer goes out, be prepared to start taking calls. Keep in mind that the average person needs to see something 7 times before it sinks in so don't think you are going to get a 100% call return on one mailing. Some areas that are more distressed get a lot more return calls simply because it is an area that's hard to sell and the economic growth in that area has yet to take back off.

Once you acquire your list, I would suggest mailing the same list - returned mail, of course - at least 3 times twice a year and one BIG in your face mailer after the first of the New Year. This gives you the 7 visual touches and the Big New year mailer is the one that hits them because it reminds them they have another year of taxes to pay, more insurance and upkeep, and they may finally decide to let the property go and give you a call.

If you choose to do direct mail in house meaning you are doing all the mailing. You can create a letter that is quick and to the point. If you put too many words on it, the seller will stop reading it and if you make it look like a flier or too formal, they will just think its advertisement and throw it in the trash.

We recommend using brightly colored paper to print your letter on. Then once it's on the dining room table or desk, the seller will keep seeing it because of the brightly colored paper and keep moving it around for later use. Giving it a stand out feel makes the letter seem special, and psychologically, they just don't want to throw it away. If you use matching envelopes that stand out in the mailbox, sellers are more likely to open it if it looks fun.

This letter says that the investor chose to put a photo of themselves but that is optional and up to you.

Here is an example:

<Name of the property owner>,

I saw your Property at <Property address>

I was driving through the neighborhood recently and saw a property I might be interested in buying.

Tax records indicate you are the current owner. I hope this letter finds you well.

I am sending this letter to see if you are interested in selling the home at the address above? I do not need a new loan, I can pay cash and can buy the house in as-is condition. I am not like any of those other letters you may have received and I am NOT a realtor looking to list your house either!

I am a serious buyer looking to help you out if you are looking or needing to sell. I buy rentals, pre-foreclosures, foreclosures, estate properties, and houses that are just not wanted. I can help people in pre-foreclosure from going into foreclosure and salvage their credit.

Please give me a call and let's talk about it – there is no obligation - just good information. I included my photo and my cell number to assure you that I am real and this is NOT a scam!

Thanks for reading my letter,

> My name
> 555-555-1212-cell

Make it believable and relevant to the seller's intelligence. If you oversell your interest, they may just overlook it.

<u>Car magnets</u> - This is highly effective for everyday visual impact. A car magnet can be placed on the doors of the vehicle, the back tailgate, or the bed of

a pickup and can be moved from vehicle to vehicle. Keep this super simple and clear to read since it will be seen in traffic situations. You want people to see what you do and get a phone number easily. If you add a bunch of photos and words, it becomes hard to read unless you are parked in a parking lot. Making it plain white or a solid color with a contrasting word color is a good combination and adding a phone number is best. You can simply put - We buy Houses and your phone number. Just remember you have this on your vehicle so people will take photos of it and stop you at times to ask questions. Also, if you happen to drive aggressively or experience road rage, your phone number is right there for all to see so set a good example for yourself and your business.

Car magnets can be ordered online or at a local printing shop. Or you can find kits for magnets in craft stores or variety shops as well.

Apparel
Wearing your marketing can be fun and no matter

where you go, people will see your information.

This does not have to be a form of marketing that breaks the bank. It can be economical and easy to obtain. Basic t-shirts can be purchased anywhere and at a reasonable price. You may even want to check out your local open-air markets or flea markets as more and more clothing vendors have booths and you can pick up quality t-shirts, hoodies, polos, and more for a fraction of the cost of department stores. You can create a logo, slogan, or simply put the same info as on your car magnet on the back of the shirt. Polo shirts can be a dressier marketing piece and the info can go on the front pocket area. Jackets and hats are also good for geographical areas where there may be adverse weather. You can even select a specific shirt color for your contractors and labor workers to wear so that they are advertising for you. Apparel is a form of marketing that you buy once but that you can reuse every day and it gives you a return.

This is also a great conversation starter. Since you

are wearing your marketing, people will ask you what you do, how you do it, and it gives you a chance to give a quick pitch and hand out a business card just in case they may need your services at some point.

Bandit Signs

You have seen the countless yellow and black signs at intersections and along roads saying "we buy houses any condition and a phone number". These are called Bandit Signs. Although they can be annoying and seem like its something everyone is doing, they are one of the most effective ways to bring in sellers. The fact that someone takes the time to stop and get the information off the sign and calls indicates a high level of motivation to sell.

Typically, the signs that generate the most interest are the yellow signs that are handwritten. We Buy Houses Any Condition 555-555-1212. Nothing more nothing less. Written this way, by hand, is time-consuming, but it also gives the impression of a local person who just wants to buy a house. The pre-printed signs and the ones with 800 numbers scream big business and people who are in distress and need to sell oftentimes think big business is just going to take advantage of them so they avoid calling them.

The main thing with these signs is placement. A lot of towns and municipalities have setbacks from intersections or permits required to place signs. Learn your area if you wish to place in town. Something to keep in mind is that outside city limits the restrictions generally fall away. You want to place the sign in the ground on what is called an "H" stick. It is a wire stand that looks like the letter "H". The 2 top pieces slide into the sign and the bottom 2 into the ground. You can also hang Bandit signs on telephone poles or make your own stand for them. Just make sure that you place them in a visible area, not overgrown by grass and brush. It is good practice to pick up signs after a while and move them around. This also allows you to remove signs that have faded and are no longer legible. This also lets you track where your signs get the most attention.

Once your signs are placed, you should start getting calls. People will call multiple numbers on those signs to see who will help them the best. So, make sure you answer the call because the one who answers is typically the one who gets the deal.

Free Online Ads

Using free classified sites to advertise that you buy houses can give you exposure to a group of people who maybe don't get out as often as others and that use the internet for most of their needs. Sites like Craigslist are free to list an ad and can let you post in many areas at one time. This marketing can flare up and make more decorative and detailed. Since you have a captive audience sitting and reading the ad, you can add a photo or a more descriptive outline of what you are looking to buy or how you can help them sell that unwanted property.

Make sure that you don't make promises that you

cannot keep - like we WILL buy your house in 30 days or less. Rather, say we CAN buy your house in 30 days or less. The word WILL implies a certain action and the word CAN imply a possible action. Keep the Ad clean and clear and make sure how they can contact you is visible and not buried in the verbiage of the Ad. Place variations of the ad in the same location using different styles and photos because different people are attracted to different styles of print advertising.

In conjunction with posting Ads online, you can search houses for sale by owner and call them to see if the property they have fits your criteria or the criteria of any of your buyer clients.

Website Landing Page

Website landing pages are a great way to have a web presence that does not require a full-blown web site. Unless you are selling a multi-tiered service to a client, a landing page is the best way to go.

This is a 1-page website that people can visit, read a brief blurb about what you do, fill out a form for you to get back to them and click send. The form comes to your inbox and you follow up with them.

Setting up a page is fairly easy but getting traffic to it can be a bit more challenging. You need to use Search Engine Optimization(SEO) strategies to get your page to show up at the top of searches and you need to set up ways for people to be diverted to your page to generate leads. This may require enlisting the assistance of web tech and this may cost a small fee to have them help.

You can promote your page anywhere you do marketing as well. Add it your business card, your apparel, your classified ads - this gives people an alternative to calling you upfront and it gives you a way to respond to them via email as well.

Find Bank-Owned Properties

Bank-owned properties are properties where the

owners have defaulted on the mortgage payments and the bank has foreclosed on the mortgage note and the bank now owns the property. Since banks are not in the business of owning real estate, they do not like to keep these on their books very long. But, oftentimes, foreclosures fall through the cracks because of all the legal hoops the banks need to jump through to foreclose. There are different stages where the property can and cannot be resold. Locating a property in this window of available time can be challenging, but once you build a relationship with a bank, they can call you when a property has been or is going to be foreclosed on and see if it fits your criteria.

To get started on locating bank-owned properties, go to your preferred search engine and type in the city you want to search in and the word "bank". At least 15 pages of banks will come up in your desired city and the surrounding areas. Write down all the banks with less than 3 locations or banks with the word "community" in the name. If you don't recognize the name of the bank, then write it down along with the phone number. Then write down the rest of the banks on the pages to call as well. Make sure you write down at least 25 banks, to begin with, along with their name and phone number. After calling all 25, write down 25 more and continue this process.

When you call the bank and the receptionist answers the phone, ask for the person in charge of REO assets (foreclosures). When the person in charge of REO assets answers the phone, say

*"Hi, my name is _____ and I am or I work for a real estate investor that buys a lot of properties in this local area. We were looking to see if you have any properties that you are looking to sell that are **not** listed on the MLS."*

If they say no, thank them for their time and move on.

If they say yes, ask them the following questions or give them your email so they can send you more information regarding the property, especially if they have multiple properties to sell. If you go the email route, be sure to get the name and extension of the person you spoke to so you can follow up if the email is not received or you have questions or if a property meets your criteria.

Questions to Ask:

Address of the property: _____

Asking price: _____

Lockbox code (way to enter the property so we can inspect): _____

Bank Name and Address: _____

Contact Name and Phone Number: _____

Email Address: _____

Is the Property for sale: yes or no

If it is for sale, what does the bank want to sell it for_____

If it is not for sale, what are your options as an investor who may be interested in buying it_____

Banks will sell the property for less than market value because they don't want it, cannot manage a rental, and do not want to maintain a property. They may also sell it for less than the original mortgage value was just to move it along.

Banks are more apt to sell at a discount toward the end of the fiscal year as well because it reflects negatively on their earnings records so pay special attention to the end of year foreclosure sales.

Real Estate Professionals

Real estate brokers and agent always have inventory they have not listed yet. They hold on to it because it may not be a market-worthy property or the seller has not yet said to list it. So, it is great to attend events or reach out to real estate professionals asking them for pocket listings.

This form of generating properties for cashflow takes building a relationship and some performance on your end. So you need to not only reach out to brokers and agent but you will need to follow up and stay in touch.

If you do not know any real estate professionals, then you need to take some time to call around to the local Real Estate offices and ask the receptionist in the office who deals with investment properties or investors. Talking to the receptionist is always best as this person has the greatest handle on who does what in the office. By doing this, you are making 1 call to be transferred to that person not making 15 calls asking each realtor if they are the person in the office that can help you. Once you make contact with that person, just have a conversation. Let them know you are an investment buyer and you are looking to work with an agent to find more properties. Ask them what they think of the investment market in the area. Is there a specific neighborhood that seems to sell faster than others? Do they get a lot of distressed properties to list? Whatever you feel, you need to ask to help find out if this person may be able to help you. Brokers and agents can be very busy but you should still offer to sit and have coffee with them to talk about how to work with them.

It helps if you get them some buying criteria to keep in mind. This lets them know you are serious about buying something because you have taken the time to write down what you prefer. If you have cash or have buyers with cash, you just need to tell them you are a cash buyer and can close in with "X" number of days if they can bring you a good opportunity. You want to emphasize with them that you are not looking for properties that are already on the market. Those properties have already been seen by all the other investors and potential buyers and you want things that are not out on the open market. There is no need to tell them you are going to wholesale or double close the property. If that is your plan, as many brokers and real estate agent are not familiar with the unconventional ways, investors buy properties. Present yourself confidently as the actual buyer because you are just that - the buyer.

Once an agent brings you a property, you will need to adhere to the legal parameters of the real estate process and the real estate professional may need to list it once you have agreed to buy it and that is ok. Since most real estate professionals can't earn their commission unless the property is listed for sale, you want to make sure they get compensated for helping you find the great deal you are about to close on. This will entail a legal state-recognized purchase agreement provided by the Broker/Agent, a closing process through an attorney or Title company, and to wire funds for closing. this does not mean you need to wait to assign the contract or set up a double close situation. It just means that on the first half of your transaction, an agent will be involved but not in the second part of the closing.

If meeting face to face is not how you want to run your initial marketing for properties with brokers and agent, then send them a letter. Introduce yourself. Let them know you are interested in buying and what you would like to buy. You can send out postcards or letters whatever you feel represents you best. Once they get the letter, you can do a follow-up call and verbally introduce yourself and see if they are receptive to speaking to you further. If not, move on to the next person.

There are so many types of real estate professionals you can reach out to that it's not worth forcing a relationship with someone who is not interested in worrying with you. Do not be offended and keep following up. The right person will surface and you will be able to do many deals together.

Real Estate Investment Clubs

Every investor at one point in their investment career should belong to a real estate investment club. These clubs can be a wealth of knowledge and a great source for finding properties. Just like you, the other members are looking for or offering investment properties up for sale.

Working with other investors through this avenue

can help you find more creative ways to buy and sell investments and can help you hone your skills as a buyer and a seller.

Investment clubs typically meet once a month and offer a specific training topic related to real estate, real estate investing, or highlight service providers that help investors further their businesses. Meeting with like-minded individuals and conducting transactions can help you build a buyer's list for future investments and can help you find other wholesalers who search for and secure properties for you to buy.

Community Organizations

Everyone at one point has a property to sell. Whether it is their personal property or an estate or rental, there is always a deal to find so put yourself in areas and situations that allow you to meet people of all areas of your community. If there is a specific neighborhood you favor, join the neighborhood club and become an active member in that community.

Becoming involved in your community activities gives you a better sense of what is happening around you, helps you discover new neighborhoods you might prefer and can help you learn who lives there and what is and may become available. Once people in the community learn who you are and what you do and see that you are making an effort to contribute to the positive growth of the area, they will start to approach you with opportunities that could bring good cash flow.

Also being mindful of community development and neighborhoods that your city will be investing in can be an asset. If you visit a city development site or community planning meeting, you will learn inside information about growth and areas the city is going to improve before everyone else. This is a great time to start marketing in these areas and getting properties locked and purchased before the improvements happen and the market prices go up. OR you can buy at a lower price point and hold on to it until the market does go up and you can sell or keep it rented when the market is higher for a better cash flow profit. By just being involved, you will find you can have access to privileged information to move your business forward.

Tax Sale/Commissioner Sales/Auctions

The excitement of an auction can be addictive and you can get excited to win a bid on a property for pennies on the dollar. Just be careful not to get swept up in the overpaying and bidding up of investments so you need to be mindful to stick to your researched properties and the purchase threshold you set.

Tax sale auction is where property goes up for auction at a starting bid determined by the county and gives you the opportunity to buy the tax lien against the property. Tax lien states you buy the lien against the property for a winning bid amount - you go through a legal process where you or your attorney serves legal notices to individuals who owe the taxes and if they do not redeem or pay the back the tax amounts, you petition the court for a deed to the property. Each state can be different and the length of time may vary so learn your investment areas. A tax deed state is where the property is auctioned off for back tax amount and you get the deed either right away or within a very short timeframe if the taxpayer does not come forward to pay the taxes.

Commissioner sale is typically where the properties are auctioned off for the amount of the back taxes owed as the starting bid. Auction attendees can bid more than what is owed in back taxes and whoever wins the bid goes through a legal process to obtain the deed to the property.

Auctions that most investors are familiar with are the Pre-foreclosure or Foreclosure auction. This is when the homeowner has defaulted on the mortgage and the lender is auctioning off the property for a value acceptable to them to cover the outstanding balance. This auction often takes place at the court building in the local community of the property or at the property itself depending on who the auction company is and if they have more than one property to auction at a time. The winning buyer must pay cash on the spot or within the timeframe set by the auction or lender. This is typically not more than 30 days. The winning bidder must come forward with a viable form of payment to secure the deed transfer and pay off the bid amount or they risk being charged penalties for non-performance. Rarely does the lender transfer over the mortgage to a new individual and allow them to just take overpayments. Once the investment is paid for, you can do what you wish with the property.

The upside of auctions is you can pick up investment properties for well below market value and turn them into cash flowing investments for a good price. The downside is that you often do not get to view the property to assess the interior condition or what level of rehab may be needed. You are at the mercy of your gut instinct, your knowledge of the neighborhood, what the outside condition is, and what the potential resale value of a property may be. Then you can estimate a range of rehab expectations so that you can do your best to turn that auction into a profitable investment.

Minus the auction options, you have the opportunity to speak to someone about the property beforehand. This is one area that most investors struggle. While it may sound odd that someone would spend the time and effort to gain access to properties than not follow through, it happens more than you might expect. The fact that there is so much training on how to find the property but not much on what to do when you find one where the bottleneck occurs.

This next section is how to interact with a potential seller, and at the end of this chapter, there will be a few questions for you to ask to pre-qualify a property.

When someone responds to your marketing or

brings you a prospective property to consider, kindly open up with a general conversation about the property. Do not jump right into the cost factor or what is wrong with the property, let the seller tell you about the house. At the end of the day, this is something they, at one time, had pride in or lived in or their family lived in so be respectful when talking to them.

A general example of how the conversation could go is:

"Hi, my name is _____ and I am returning your call. (Be conversational) Or Hey, Thanks for calling me back…I sent you a letter because I see that you have a property at _____ for sale or a house that looked vacant that maybe you would be interested in selling. OR I buy properties in your area and I saw your house and it piqued my interest. I was wondering if you could tell me a little about the property. (let them talk about the house). Okay. Great, thanks, how long has the house been vacant? Are the utilities on and everything functioning properly? Did taxes pay up? Any liens that you are aware of? Can you tell me what types of repairs or updates the house may need? (this is the seller's time to devalue the property. It helps them verbally and mentally realize the amount of work that may need to be done. Also, this helps you make note of how much it may cost to repair the property). If you used it as a rental, how much were you getting a month if you don't mind me asking? What were you hoping to get for the property dollar-wise? Ok, well let me tell you what I'm going to do. I'll drive by again and walk around (if vacant), run my numbers, and I'll call you back in about 24-48 hours and set a time to go inside or let you know if it is going to work for me. Is there anything more you think I need to know? Thanks again for taking the time to tell me about your property. I'll be sure to give you a callback."

Of course, this is an example with a few scenarios, so make it your own. But you see how the dialog is friendly and open. You are interested in the property as a potential investment so you need as much information as you can get. You want them to feel good about selling you the property so make them feel good and let them tell the story. The more you talk to sellers, the easier it is to converse with them and not feel like you are questing them.

Never offer a price on the spot, especially if you have not seen the actual property. Always do a drive-by first then set a physical meeting. This puts the ball in your court and you control the transaction. When you set up a time to view the inside, you should have already determined what you could pay for the property based off the conversation with the seller regarding the condition of the house, the market values you determined in the area, and what you might plan to do with the investment. Again, no need to offer a price at this time either. Walk the inside and take a closer look at what rehab the property needs and take notes. Feel free to ask about certain areas of disrepair that are obvious like a roof that has been patched and what happened to cause that leaky roof or pipe break?

The more you walk properties, the more you will learn what to ask about and what not to ask about because you already know the answer, and although you want to gather as much info as possible, you don't want the seller to feel bad about the condition of the property since they may live in, have lived in it, or a relative lived in it.

After the walk-through assessments, tell them you will call them in 24 hours and let them know if the deal will work for you. Try not to say I'll call with my offer or I will call and tell you what I am willing to pay. These can put people on the defensive and that is not what you want. Then be sure to call back and let them know if the property will work for you or not. If it does not work, be honest and explain that for your business model, the rehab would be too much for you to make a profit or that their anticipated asking price plus the rehab would put the property over market value and you would not be able to resell it for a profit. If the property could be a good investment and you want to make an offer, let them know the offer and any supporting information you have to justify the price point. You may even want to show them what other distressed properties have sold for in that area to help them see that the number you are offering is fair and comparable to other properties you could buy instead.

If you both agree, set a time to meet and get the purchase agreement signed right away. Then you are able to move forward with your investment model. If you wait too long, the seller may shop around for someone else to buy the property and you could lose the deal altogether. So, do not wait. Real estate transactions are happening every day, several times a day, each day of the week so those who wait can miss out on a great deal.

The next page is a worksheet of general questions you could ask a seller to pre-qualify a property. Use this as a stepping stone to creating a more detailed worksheet as you grow and gain more experience.

Seller Information Sheet

Property Address:_____

How did you hear about me?
_____

Seller's name:
_____

Seller's phone/Email:
_____

Type of Property:
- Single Family
- Multi-Family
- Mobile
- Commercial

Number of Beds: _____

Baths: _____

Garage: _____

Basement: _____

Sq Footage of livable space:_____

Year Build:_____

Lot size:_____

What repairs may be needed:

_____

_____

_____

Is there a mortgage or liens on the property:

_____ $$ amount _____

Taxes current: _____

How much are taxes: _____

Is the property occupied: _____

By Owner or Tenant: _____

If tenant, how much is rent:_____

Lease and length of lease: _____

How much would you like to get for the property_____

Notes:

_____

_____

_____

_____
_____
_____

_____

Offer Price: _____
ARV:_____
Est rehab:_____
Close Date:_____

Use this as a starting point for conversation. After a while, you will be able to work all of these questions and more in general conversation with the seller and it will not even appear that you are filling out a questionnaire.

Overcoming Challenges and Quitting Your Day Job

With every endeavor, you will not be an expert right away. There will be a learning curve and you will learn to develop your own flair for real estate investments based on your area of preference, location of investments, and your personality. Along with this learning curve will come challenges. So please do not expect that it will be smooth sailing and that every deal will be golden.

Some challenges can easily be overcome and some you may not overcome and lose a deal. But if you remain logical and not emotional, you can work through it and set up systems to avoid that in the future.

Let's talk about a few challenges that some investors have experienced and what the result was. These are not meant to scare you away from investing but to give you an idea that all investors go through challenges and that they can overcome them.

Can't find an end buyer for a wholesale opportunity

If you don't have a solid buyer's list and you get a property under contract, you may struggle to assign it to someone. With each purchase agreement, you should make sure that you have several contingencies in place to allow you to bow out of an opportunity if you can't make the deal happen after all.

One of the most important contingencies is an inspection clause. You typically want no less than 10 business days to inspect the property. During this time, you will be able to assess rehab and locate an end buyer for the investment. If by chance you cannot locate a buyer, you can cancel the option to buy due to the fact that the property did not meet your inspection parameters. Make sure that the purchase agreement allows you to inspect the property with an inspector or contractor as the amount of rehab may prohibit the deal from offering the cash flow needed as well.

Another good contingency is partner approval. Make the deal contingent on your partner's approval, that way if you cannot find a partner to buy the deal from you and you can say your partner does not approve, you can request to cancel.

Just make sure that whatever contingency you include, it's something that makes sense and can be easily proven.

Farmhouse

An investor finds an old farmhouse that needs repair. The seller got married, the new wife does not want to live in the old run-down property so it's being sold by the owner for a lower than market value. The investor assesses the property, determines the flip value and what rehab is needed, and makes the deal happen.

The investor invites an engineer to the property to design an addition to the house that will bring it up to current living standards and desires for the neighborhood. A new addition is created and approved by the city and the investor hires a licensed contractor to do the work.

The project gets going and everything is looking good. The contractor is buzzing along and comes to the part of the project where the old house and the new addition are put together by the roofline. The old house wall is removed and the roof cut back to join the new roof and the contractor missed a piece in the plans and the roof is 2 feet too low to meet the existing roofline of the house.

This will now require the new roof to be totally removed and redone to the drawing standard and then reroofed so the project can continue. This is an expensive mistake and one the contractor should absorb. What happens now? This will cost the investor time, construction loan payments, a delay in the rest of the project which may cause the project go into the winter season, and put a hold on finishing the exterior before the weather hits. The project now becomes overwhelming and the investor is stuck.

The inspector cannot do anything because even though the roof is framed too low, the framing is done to code so no violation could be imposed unless it actually was connected to the existing structure. Because of this, the insurance company won't pay out because there is really no violation. The contractor has now walked away because you cannot afford to redo the entire addition and the property sits vacant and open to the elements. Do you feel this investor's pain?

Your options are to spend more money and go after the contractor in civil court to get the funds to fix the issues. But you have no guarantee that the contractor has the money to give you. So you lose in this option no matter what. You can hire a new contractor to redo all the work at your expense or you can consider talking to the lender and seeing what your options are to extend or worse - be foreclosed on.

The investor here fought the insurance company and the contractor and won less than 5,000 because there were no code violations, And even though the contractor walked off the job, there were no provisions for him not completing the job other than he would not receive his contracted pay. The investor negotiated with the lender and ended up surrendering the house back to the lender for the lender to sell – this is called a deed in lieu, meaning in lieu of paying the loan the property was surrendered as payment.

This is an extreme case but the investor could not recover the cost of the challenge to make the project right and would have spent a month fighting it in court to gain nothing of substance to rectify the issue. So here they decided to walk away and cut their losses. The best choice for all parties involved.

Quit Claim Deed Liens

When purchasing a property via quitclaim deed, the investor acquires not only the property but any and all liens and judgments against the property. In this example, the investor found a property that would create good monthly cash flow and that they could purchase the property for a low price. A quitclaim deed purchase was best because closing costs would have equaled the purchase price. The investor decided to conduct a title search to ensure the property title was clean and could be transferred without issues. The title company conducted a title search and found $109,000.00 in IRS liens against the property. The house value was only $40,000.00. Clearly, the house could not be sold without the IRS taking the sale funds and the investor is stuck with the outstanding balance.

After further investigation, the title company found that the IRS had inadvertently placed the lien on the property. The liens were from someone with the exact name and since data entry is human-driven, someone had put a lien on the wrong property. The seller was able to prove to IRS it was not their lien and the liens were removed and the sale closed. The investor here could have walked away and not bothered with it but because they took the extra step to overcome the challenge, they were able to get the liens removed, purchase the property for a low price, and rent it out for $850.00 a month making positive cash flow.

Just because there was a challenge didn't mean it could not be overcome to make the deal a profitable win for the investor.

Unforeseen Rehab

Undoubtedly, there will be times that an investor buys a property, does a walkthrough, and thinks they have a good handle on the rehab. Then you open a wall to repair plumbing and you find that you have dry rot in the wall and you need to remove the drywall and replace wall studs. Obviously, not an exciting find in a wall but one you cannot ignore.

The investor here has options 1) add more to the

budget and reduce the profit margin or 2) adjust the budget numbers and reconsider a lower grade of granite to offset the wall repair.

What would you do? The decision does not have to be earth-shattering but you need to step back and look at the options and make a logical decision to best meet the outcome goal set at the beginning of the project. In this case, the investor adjusted the granite selection and came in on budget and met the anticipated profit margin.

Bad Contractors

Working with other people on a project can be a challenge in that 1) it's not their project, 2) it's not their money, and 3) their way of working may not align with yours. Therefore, there can be conflict very easily.

If you do rehab, you will come across unreliable labor from time to time. There are ways to try to combat this by using contracts that offer penalties for not reaching deadlines. Make sure you collect their insurance and bond information upfront so they know if they do not perform, you can go after them legally and make sure that you or a representative is present onsite on a regular basis and at random times to ensure that someone is working on the project. But even with all that, some contractors are just not reliable and they flounder from job to job not upholding a standard of quality or service.

One way to safeguard yourself from a challenge like this is to regulate the compensation for work completed. Set up a compensation schedule in accordance with the timeframe of the project. If you are paying for materials, there is no need to pay upfront for work not completed so no deposit is needed. Pay for completed work only, and if you can help it, do not pay with cash. If a contractor walks away, you have the ability to recover anything. Legally, a cash trail never goes anywhere and you cannot prove you paid them.

Don't give a contractor too much room to fail. If

they cease showing up for a job, then the job needs to move on without them. Have more than 1 crew available to you in case something happens. If a contractor has been unseen or unheard from for 2-3 days and their crew has not completed any work - reach out to them to set a time for them to get their tools and bring in a new crew. Time is money and this is YOUR business and they work for you. You control the flow of work and the progress and if someone slacks off or goes AWOL, replace them and move on.

Rogue Partners

Having partners in a real estate environment can be very beneficial. But if the partnership is not spelled out clearly and roles defined in writing, one can try to rise above and overstep their role causing conflict within the partnership.

In one instance, a few real estate investors joined forces on a multi-family living property. Things were good for a while and business was progressing. Not as quickly as they had planned and the property needed some un-projected repairs so the profit was less than expected monthly and some months there was no profit the first year. The partners, as you can imagine, became frustrated and decided to hire an outside source to help manage the property. One of the out-of-state partners took it upon themselves to dictate the role of the manager and ask them to perform tasks outside the original scope of the agreement. Not being local, they did not have a grasp on the needs but continues to try to overstep and approve things they know nothing about. They began asking the manager to pay for things that the other partners were unaware of such as taxes, insurance, and mortgage payments. These items had already been set up by the CPA to be paid automatically so asking the manager to do this too caused funds to be held back and items to be overpaid. This made the partnership look disorganized and caused further confusion and delay in making the investment positive cash flowing property.

When the rogue partner was confronted, they became defensive and began calling all the service providers they had in common complaining about the team and trying to divide the other members from the service providers they used in their private investments. When the other partners found out about these efforts to divide the team, they came together and reviewed the partnership agreement. They decided that the partnership could not remain as it was any longer. They consulted an attorney and decided to buy out the rogue partner and part ways. They presented the rogue partner with his initial investment plus a small return for his percentage of the year's income received and they terminated their partnership with that individual.

While no one wants a partnership to fail, it happens. Minimizing the damage to the overall investment and the other members involved has to be the primary consideration. All the partners here could have gone rogue and tried to push the issues and talk bad about one another but it took them taking a step back, reviewing the agreement, and making an educated decision to make the change needed to improve the situation.

As you can see, there will always be challenges that come up in life and in real estate investing it is no different. No matter how much you plan and try to make it flow smoothly, there are things that just come up that need extra attention. All you can do is try to be as prepared as you can. Use contracts written by professionals, make partnership agreements as clear as you can, and always include a contingency buffer in your rehab numbers. These may not eliminate a challenge from occurring but it can minimize the damage that can be caused when a challenge does arise. Overcoming challenges is part of the business and if you go back to the beginning and remember "WHY". You are doing this in the first place, those challenges won't bother you as much.

Quitting Your Day Job

More than likely you got into real estate investing so

that if you work a regular job, you can quit at some point and live life on your terms. This is a reality and one that does not need to take years and years to achieve. During your goal setting portion of the business set up, you wrote down some personal goals. If firing your boss was one of them, then you should have outlined the process you needed to make that happen.

Deciding to do real estate full time right from the beginning is not recommended. It can take time to build up cash flow and get deals closed, and if you eliminate the regular paycheck right away or too soon, you may find yourself struggling needlessly.

Setting up a timeframe to quit your day job should not be taken lightly. You need to look at all the benefits of having a regularly paying job. You likely get benefits of some sort and incentives or bonuses that you have counted on for regular financial survival. Going all-in in real estate to soon and eliminating those perks can catch you off guard. if you get sick and no longer have health insurance but have not been able to get a real estate transaction completed, you may not have the money to pay for the medical treatment needed - if you have children, this can be devastating. You need to look at the big picture.

While real estate investing can be life-changing, it is not a get-rich-quick option. It takes time to generate leads, find buyers, and close on investments. If you go the rental property route, you may experience tenant that doesn't pay and if you are relying on that monthly rent to support yourself and it does not come in, that can hurt you financially. If you need to evict someone that takes money and if you are not supplementing your efforts, you could lose more than your sanity. Bad real estate deals and loss of money can destroy your esteem, your desire to try again, and that can put stress on you, your family, or in an extreme case, cause you to lose your own home. So setting up a plan before you give your 2-week notice is essential.

Planning to quit your job should consider your current income status and how to transition out of that daily grind. If you make sufficient money in your job to cover your bills and everyday living, you will want to make sure that you at least are consistently bringing in a minimum of that much money every month.

I would strongly suggest that you look at the lifestyle you would like to have. How much income do you need to generate each month to live THAT life? Likely the life you would like to have is more expensive than the life you have today. A bigger house, nicer cars, college tuitions, being able to set up programs to give back to the community, or ??? If you are not financially sustaining these things now, then you will need more money to do that in the future. So when planning to quit your job, make sure that you are prepared financially to sustain the life you want to have. This also allows a buffer so that if something should not go as planned, then you should still have enough cash flow to cover a life that is comfortable.

Also, and I know you have heard this before, do not live within your means. What this is saying is that if your monthly cash flow is $15,000.00, do not live a life that costs $15,000.00 a month. Put money away for taxes, buy a less expensive car, and don't overextend on your personal residence. Now that you are a business owner, you will need to pay your own income taxes and taxes on your investment cash flow. This can be a real shocker when tax time comes and you had a great year but failed to set aside funds to pay your taxes. This bill alone could eat up a couple months' earnings very easy. Also, make sure you are not overextending yourself on credit card debt. If you can afford to pay cash for it, then you can't afford it. If you can't live without this item, do some more deals to pay for it.

Financing cars, boats, RV type toys, and extravagant lifestyles can cost you more than you realize in interest rates and fees. If you MUST finance something, make sure that the income you are generating from that investment can cover the monthly finance fee. If you finance a vehicle, make sure it's a vehicle that will bring you a return. Just be smart about the things you choose to include in your life and remember your "WHY". If you get sucked in by the glamor of a life that can cause you to go off track, none of the effort you have put out is worth it.

We are not saying that real estate investment lifestyles cannot be rewarding and you cannot reap the fruit of your efforts. Please enjoy the dream vacation, p for your child's dream wedding, and buy the car of your dreams. Just be mindful that when considering the early retirement option, consider who you are, what you need, and what you can afford to give up. Do not short change the process. You set the pace in your business and maybe you can replace or exceed your income in 6 months but maintaining that may take 6 more months. Don't feel like you need to rush into being a full-time real estate investor. Set yourself up to succeed.

Conclusion

Here we are at the final overview of all the wonderful information you have just been fed. If you feel like you have been drinking from a firehose, go back and reread some of the sections that seem overwhelming or that you want to really digest. Use this book as a systematic approach to engaging in real estate investing for cash flow a reality for you.

This book has been written for you and the hopes that you are able to take the information in here and internalize it and make it work for you in your geographic area so that you can become the successful real estate investor you knew you could be.

If we look at the book as a whole, use this as a tool that you will be able to use to set yourself up on the right road.

We have looked at ways to set up your business entity and ways to make sure that what you are setting up reflects what you want to do. We shared many ways to market yourself so that you can start generating lists of leads to buy investment properties and lists of people to sell them too. We looked at many different ways to generate cash flow and learned that no one way is the same for each investor. Opening up the thought that every real estate investor encounters challenges, but with the right outlook and a calm approach, you can find a way through the challenges and meet the needs of all parties involved. Finally, we realized that the potential to quit your job can be a reality with the right planning and efforts.

While real estate investing is not rocket science, it can require just as much thought and planning. Making sure that all the pieces of the puzzle are in place to visualize the whole image of success is easy when you have a blueprint or a path to follow already forged by other investors.

Earlier in the book, we mentioned that fear is a liar. It comes in to steal your confidence and tries to overshadow the knowledge you have to complete a deal and make consistent cash flow. When fear arrives at your mind's door, you can do one of 2 things 1) Face Everything And Run or 2) Face Everything And Rise. Choose to rise up and face fear. Challenge yourself to step outside of your comfort zone and shake off the negativity you hold on to or that others throw on you that you cannot succeed in this industry in unconventional ways. Engage in as much self-preparation information you can get and implement the nuggets that resonate with you. Be kind to those who doubted you and when you succeed, do not boast and say "I told you so!", rather offer to bring them into the circle of success and bless them with the same opportunity you have been successful at.

At the end of the day, you have to know in your deep "WHY" soul that you have done right by yourself, treat others well and with respect, and that when you lay your head on your pillow at night, you gave a 100% effort to take the next step to reach your goals. We know that in times of trouble, you will take steps backward - come back to this book and regroup. Begin again. The great thing about investing in real estate is that there is always another deal to be done so remembering that a failed deal today means you are closer to complete the deal tomorrow.

We want to thank you for making it through to the end of *Real Estate for Cash Flow - How to Create Cash Flow and Wealth Through Real Estate Investments.*

We are confident in saying that we know from personal experience real estate investing can change your life and we hope you found the book informative and we were able to provide you with all of the tools you need to achieve your goals whatever they may be.

Because we believe you can succeed, we are offering you a special surprise. The next section is an AMAZING BONUS MATERIALS section. This information, forms, ad examples, scripts, and ideas can help you move along easier and can help you reach your goals faster.

Enjoy the next chapter of your life in real estate investing and we hope to see you in some of the investment circles in your area someday.

BONUS MATERIALS

<u>Using Craigslist to find deals:</u>
- Go to Craigslist.com
- Choose where you want to research properties
- Under "housing", click on real estate for sale
- Refine the search by choosing "by-owner"
- Then, in the search box at the top of the page, type keywords that would be reflective of a distressed property. Along with your keyword, also type in the city that you want to buy in because Craigslist covers multiple cities per area
    - Anytown+fixer
- Look at the results and select an ad that meets the criteria you are looking for. Call the seller and fill out the seller sheet.

- Find the value of the property through running comps. IF the price meets your buying criteria contact seller make an offer.
- Go through the list then repeat the process but replace the keyword. Keep moving along and replace with motivated and the city name.
- Continue to this process with the following keyword examples:
  - Needs work
  - AS IS
  - Must sell
  - Handyman special
  - Fixer-upper
  - Seller finance

Ad for Rehab Crew

Real estate investment company looking for a motivated rehab crew:

- We buy many houses in _____ including foreclosures and distressed properties and we need someone to bid and rehab our local projects and work with our other team players. This is a position for independent contractors who meet all of the following criteria:

- Have a reliable mode of transportation and cellphone for job duties direction and communication.
- Having experience in construction and/or rehabbing-specialty areas are fine but prefer someone who is universally skilled
- Be able to walk through houses and determine the scope of work and expense required and put it in writing.
- Knowledge of plumbing, electrical work, roofing, and finish work
- Be knowledgeable of local code requirements (including rental code)
- Be able to work a flexible schedule to meet timelines

- Be experienced with following punch lists
- Have good organization and communication skills
- Be proficient with email, scanning, and fax
- Work without supervision and clean up after yourself
- Be willing to travel to locations in _____ counties

If you have your own crew, that's fine. We are looking for ongoing workers, not a one-and-done, so I expect pricing to reflect ongoing work as well. If you meet the above-mentioned criteria and are looking for a new, exciting, and lucrative position, please email me your contact info, qualifications, and income requirements.

<u>Contractor Interview</u>

1. What is an example of a project that you have recently completed?

2. Are you able to walk through houses and determine the scope of work and expense required?
3. Are you familiar with local code requirements (including rental code)?
4. Are you licensed bonded and insured?
5. Are you registered with the city of Gary?
6. Would you be able to work a flexible schedule to meet timelines?
7. Do you have experience in putting together punch lists for materials?
8. Do you have good organization and communication skills?
9. Are you proficient with email, scanning, and fax?
10. Are you reliable and can work independently? Meaning can you forecast yourself what needs to be done or do you prefer to work off a checklist for daily requirements?
11. Do you have reliable transportation and would you be willing to travel a minimal amount?

12. How many members are in your crew and how many jobs can you manage at one time?
13. What are your pay expectations?
14. When would you be available to start if you were selected for the team?

Free Classified Websites to consider
- Kijiji.com
- UPillar.com
- Webclassifieds.us
- Classifiedsforfree.com
- Pennysaverusa.com
- Salespider.com
- Postlets.com
- Adpost.com

Finding A-Players to be on your Team

Taking the time to hire the right person that fits the "A" player description is critical to making sure that the job will be done right and that you will not be required to spend your time micromanaging them.

The difference in hiring an "A" and "B" player is significant. It is the difference between getting deals done or not getting deals done. Some people think that hiring a "B" player vs hiring an "A" player just means the difference in how much money they will make a per deal or the number of deals they can do. There is no in-between. The difference in hiring someone putting in 99% compared to someone putting in 100% is 1000% productivity. You cannot hire a "B" player and pay them more money and expect them to perform better. Their work ethic is their work ethic.

Here are the things to look for in an "A" player:
- Always shows early
- Do what they say they are going to do and oftentimes more
- Say please and thank you
- Address you with respect
- Never has to be told twice
- You never have to follow up on their work to make sure it was done right
- Pay rate doesn't create an "A" player

- Takes little info and completes the rest by figuring things out independently
- Takes accountability and admits if they do something wrong
- Addresses problems, fixes them, then tells you what they did
- The bigger the workload, the bigger their resource fullness
- Never says "I can't" because "Can't" never did anything
- Doesn't tear others down to make themselves look better
- Has a "results" oriented attitude, not "keep busy" attitude
- Sends you updates & keeps you posted on project status without being asked
- Completes tasks on time or early

An "A" player does not see themselves as the owner of the company but is someone you would trust to run the company in your absence. Finding these people is a process, and after reading the list above, you may say you are not an "A" player.

Social Media Ad Examples

Social media ads are ads you put out to entice a seller or potential buyer to call you so you can form a relationship with them. We spoke about this type of marketing earlier and I wanted to share some examples with you that have a proven track record for other investors.

Once you get a property under contract, you can openly market it if you don't have a buyer in mind. You may place ads that look like this:

Priced Below Market
SFR 3/2
Great Neighborhood
Call today: xxx-xxx-xxxx

Fixer Upper!!!
SFR 3/2
Must sell/Motivated
Call today xxx-xxx-xxxx

Needs Roof/ Plumbing/ Electrical
3 bed/2 bath
Must sell/Desperate
Call today xxx-xxx-xxxx

These ads are not too specific but are the things investors are looking and what you look for when searching for potential investment properties online.

Now, if you are looking to build up your buyer's list, you may use ads like this:

Investors Wanted!
Buyers needed for multiple investment properties that cash-flow
Call today xxx-xxx-xxxx

Cash Buyers Wanted!!!
Cash buyers needed for fast closings on multiple investment properties
Call today xxx-xxx-xxxx

Wholesale Properties For Sale
Buyer needed. Get properties for 60% ARV. Great returns.
Call xxx-xxx-xxxx

I Need Cash Buyers!!!
I have several handyman specials.
All are 65% or more below Market Value.
I have done the work, you make the profit.
Call xxx-xxx-xxxx

As I said, these are examples and you can use the ideas to generate your own ads to reach the target market you wish to work with. Make the ad believable and do not place ridiculous rates of returns for areas. You will ruin your reputation very quickly and soon find yourself without properties to sell or buyers to buy them or you will lose both.

Letter to Real Estate Professional

Hi,

My name is _____ and I am an investor in the local area. I not only represent myself, but I also have several investors in and out of the area that I help find rehabs and rentals. I have goals to buy XXX number of properties a month and would like to know if you are interested in talking to me further.

Some of these properties I will buy and hold myself, some of them I will sell to other investors, and some I will buy, fix up, and flip. Regardless of the strategy I use, I need to be aggressive on the price I pay for the property, especially in the current market.

I have not chosen a real estate agent to represent me yet in this area. The agent that I choose cannot be afraid to offend other agents with offers that are lower than preferred. I use several strategies to buy and sell properties quickly, including making verbal offers when in time-sensitive situations. I may also look at a lot of properties and buy only a few.

The upside for the agent who gets accepted will be lots of commission. We will close on properties every month. I am a professional and I expect to work with a professional. I want to make money and I want the agent to make money. Here are the types of properties I am looking for.

Single-family homes
3-4 bedrooms
1.5-2 baths at least 1,100sqft
No mobile homes
No homes built before 1950
No vacant ground
Located in these zips:
I am looking for houses in the lower crime neighborhoods that I and my staff can be safe working at.

If you have properties fitting this description or would like to represent me, please call me at 555-555-1212.

Thank you for your time,
<Your Name>

All of these GREAT BONUS MATERIAL items are here to help you succeed and help the creative juices flow so you can set up marketing in your area. They can be retyped and reused to fit your needs and help you grow in your real estate investment business. We hope you find these as useful as they were and are still to us.

www.ingramcontent.com/pod-product-compliance
Lightning Source LLC
Chambersburg PA
CBHW070637220526
45466CB00001B/206